# An Inspector Calls

## THE GRAPHIC NOVEL
J. B. Priestley

## ORIGINAL TEXT VERSION

Script Adaptation: Jason Cobley
Linework: Will Volley
Colouring: Alejandro Sanchez
Lettering: Jim Campbell
Design & Layout: Jo Wheeler,
Jenny Placentino & Carl Andrews
Editor in Chief: Clive Bryant

An Inspector Calls: The Graphic Novel
Original Text Version
J. B. Priestley

First published: March 2012
Reprinted: September 2014, November 2015, November 2016, October 2018, January 2021
December 2022, December 2025

Published by: Classical Comics Ltd
with the permission of The Estate of J. B. Priestley
for which the publisher extends their sincere thanks.

Play copyright © J. B. Priestley 1945.
Adaptation, illustration and supporting text copyright ©2012 Classical Comics Ltd.
All rights reserved. No part of this book may be reproduced
in any form or incorporated into any information retrieval system
without the written permission of Classical Comics Ltd.

Play first published by William Heinemann Ltd 1947.

All rights whatsoever in this play are strictly reserved and applications for performances,
etc., should be made in advance by professional companies to United Agents,
12-26 Lexington Street, London W1F 0LE and by amateur companies to
Samuel French Ltd, 52 Fitzroy Street, London W1T 5JR.

Acknowledgments: Every effort has been made to trace copyright holders of
material reproduced in this book. Any rights not acknowledged here will be
acknowledged in subsequent editions if notice is given to Classical Comics Ltd.

All enquiries should be addressed to:
Classical Comics Ltd.
PO Box 177
LUDLOW
SY8 9DL
United Kingdom

info@classicalcomics.com
www.classicalcomics.com

ISBN: 978-1-906332-32-7

This book is printed by Graphy Cems, Spain using environmentally safe inks, on paper
from responsible sources. This material can be disposed of by recycling,
incineration for energy recovery, composting and biodegradation.

The rights of Jason Cobley, Will Volley, Alejandro Sanchez and Jim Campbell
to be identified as the artists of this adaptation have been asserted in accordance with
the Copyright, Designs and Patents Act 1988 sections 77 and 78.

# Contents

Dramatis Personæ ................................................ 4

## An nspector Calls

Act 1 .................................................................... 6
Act 2 .................................................................... 54
Act 3 .................................................................... 93

❖

J. B. Priestley ....................................................... 138
Page Creation ..................................................... 140

# Dramatis Personæ

Inspector Goole

Arthur Birling
*A wealthy industrialist*

Sybil Birling
*Arthur Birling's wife*

Sheila Birling
*Arthur & Sybil's daughter*

Gerald Croft
*Sheila's fiancé*

Eric Birling
*Arthur & Sybil's son*

Edna
*The Birlings' parlour-maid*

Eva Smith / Daisy Renton

LAST MONTH, JUST BECAUSE THE **MINERS** CAME OUT ON **STRIKE**, THERE'S A LOT OF **WILD** TALK ABOUT POSSIBLE **LABOUR** TROUBLE IN THE NEAR FUTURE. **DON'T** WORRY. WE'VE **PASSED** THE **WORST** OF IT.

FAIR PAY!

SAFE CONDITIONS

WE **EMPLOYERS** AT LAST ARE COMING **TOGETHER** TO SEE THAT **OUR INTERESTS** – AND THE INTERESTS OF **CAPITAL** – ARE **PROPERLY** PROTECTED.

AND WE'RE IN FOR A **TIME** OF STEADILY INCREASING PROSPERITY.

THWAK

FAIR PAY!

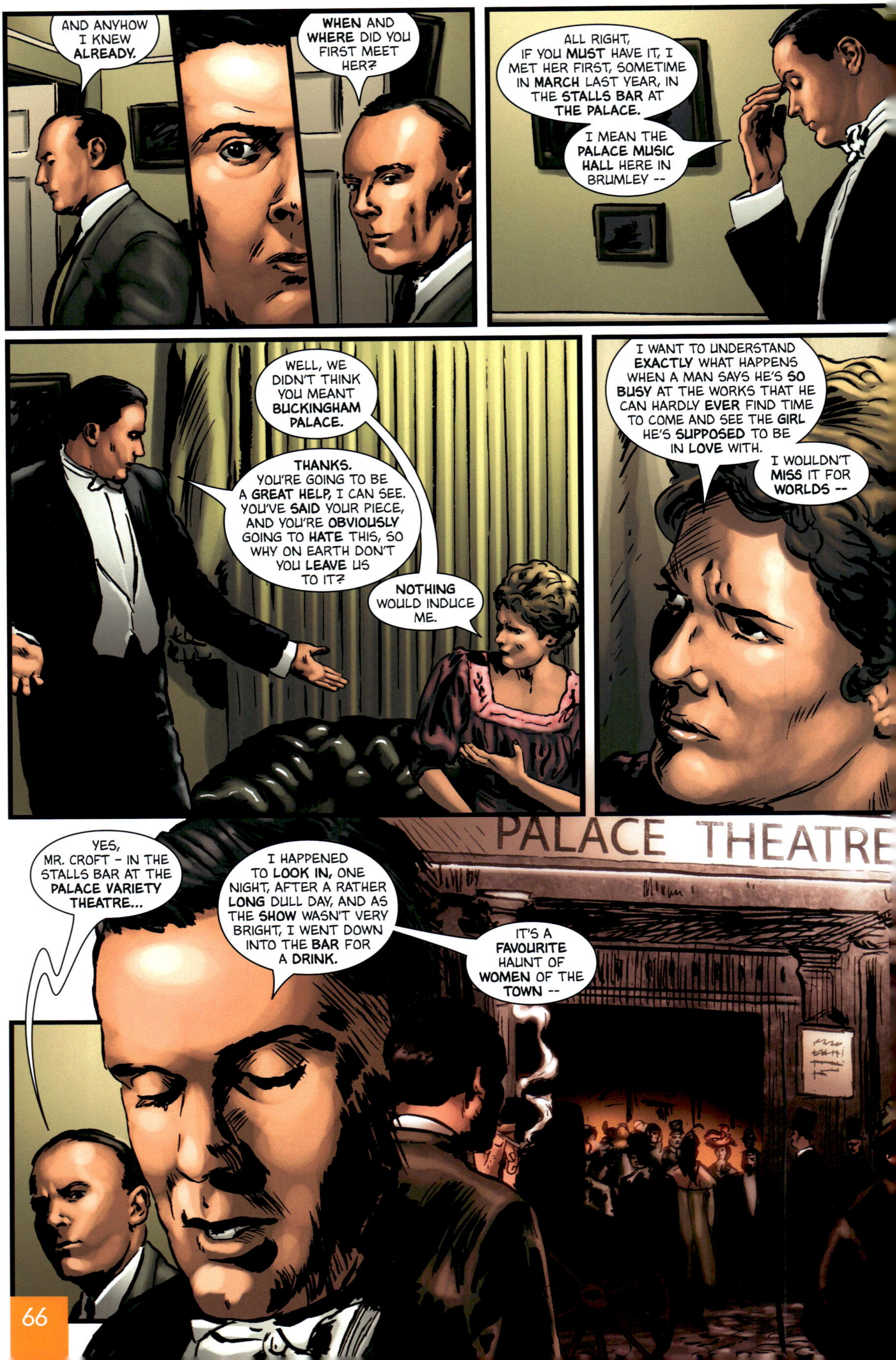

THAT'S THE STORY SHE **FINALLY** TOLD, AFTER I'D **REFUSED** TO BELIEVE HER ORIGINAL STORY – THAT SHE WAS A **MARRIED** WOMAN WHO'D BEEN **DESERTED** BY HER HUSBAND.

I DIDN'T SEE **ANY** REASON TO BELIEVE THAT **ONE** STORY SHOULD BE ANY **TRUER** THAN THE OTHER. THEREFORE, YOU'RE QUITE **WRONG** TO SUPPOSE I SHALL **REGRET** WHAT I DID.

BUT **IF** HER STORY WAS **TRUE**, IF THIS BOY **HAD** BEEN GIVING HER **STOLEN** MONEY, THEN SHE CAME TO **YOU** FOR HELP BECAUSE SHE WANTED TO KEEP THIS **YOUNGSTER** OUT OF ANY MORE **TROUBLE** – ISN'T THAT **SO**?

**POSSIBLY.** BUT IT SOUNDED **RIDICULOUS** TO ME. SO I WAS **PERFECTLY** JUSTIFIED IN ADVISING MY COMMITTEE **NOT** TO ALLOW HER CLAIM FOR ASSISTANCE.

YOU'RE NOT EVEN SORRY **NOW**, WHEN YOU KNOW WHAT **HAPPENED** TO THE GIRL?

I'M SORRY SHE SHOULD HAVE COME TO SUCH A **HORRIBLE** END. BUT I ACCEPT NO **BLAME** FOR IT AT **ALL**.

WHO IS TO BLAME THEN?

FIRST, THE GIRL HERSELF.

BLEACH
DO NOT DRINK

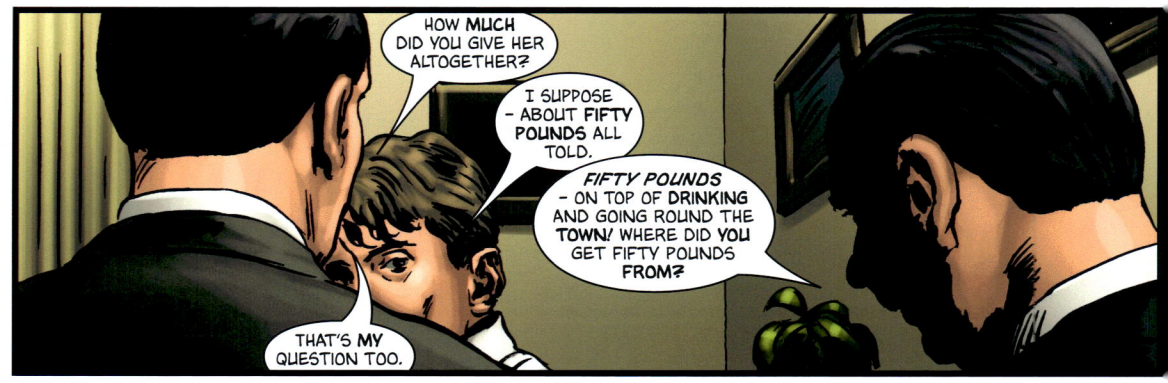

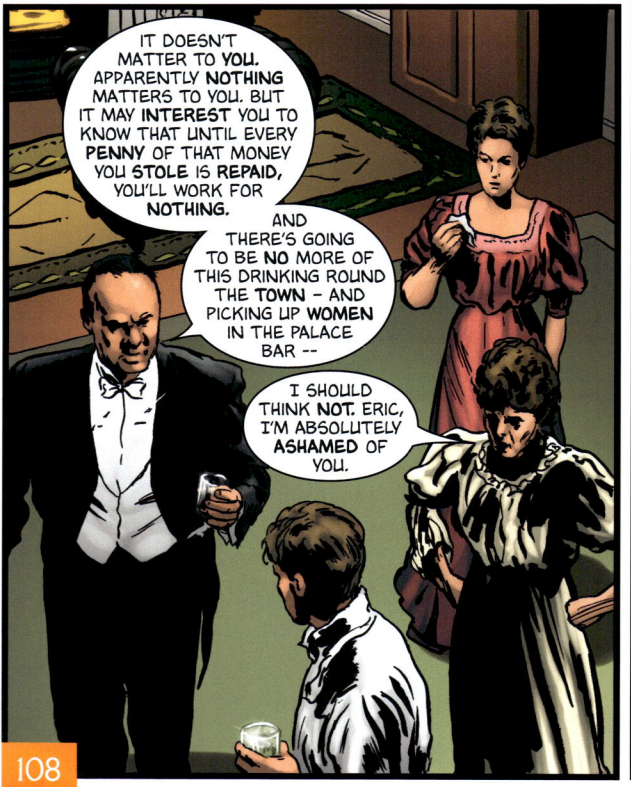

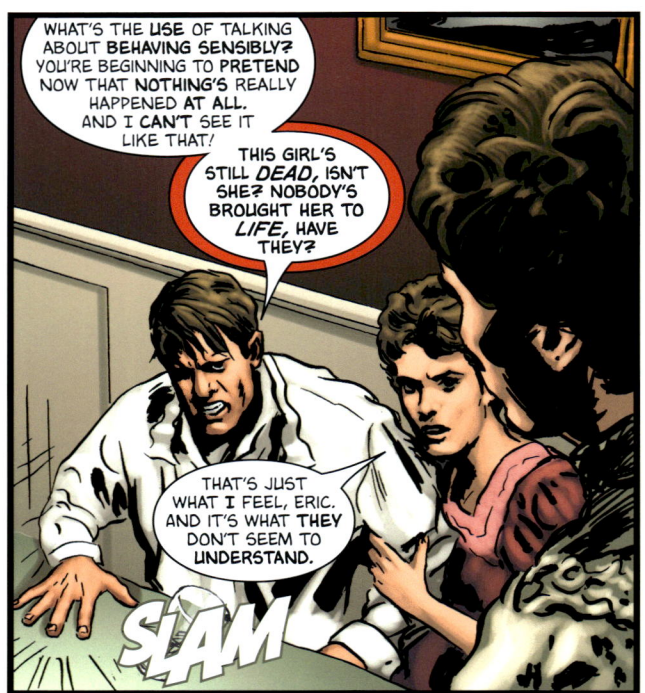

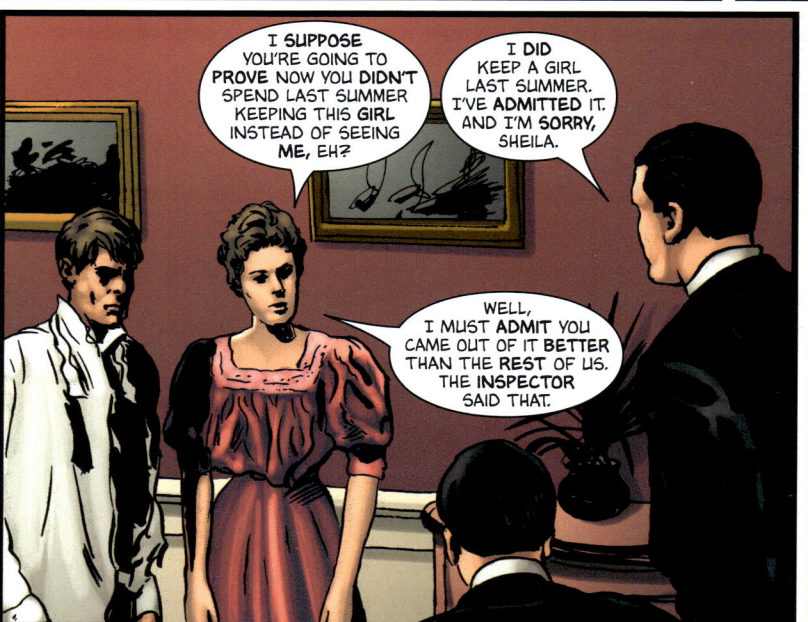

# An Inspector Calls

---

# The End

# J. B. Priestley

(1894–1984)

John Priestley (he gave himself the middle name of "Boynton" later in life) was born on 13th September 1894 in Bradford, Yorkshire. His father, Jonathan Priestley, was a schoolmaster, and his mother, Emma, had worked in a mill. Sadly, Emma died just a few months after giving birth to John, who, after his father remarried four years later, was raised by his kindly stepmother Amy.

Priestley attended Belle Vue School in Bradford and soon set his sights on writing. Although a gifted academic, he decided against going on to university, taking instead a modest office job at a local wool firm. He believed that, for a writer, life experience was more important than academic qualifications, and this office job gave him the time and freedom to pursue his literary ambitions. Far from turning his back on learning, however, he surrounded himself with books and used them to continue his education. It was also around this time that, through his father and his father's friends, Priestley became interested in socialism, a philosophy that ingrained themes and beliefs that appear throughout his works, most notably in *An Inspector Calls*.

When World War I broke out in 1914, Priestley volunteered to join the infantry. He trained for a year in the south of England before being sent to the front line in 1915. Wounded in a mortar attack in 1916, he was sent back to England for treatment and returned to the trenches six months later, only to become a victim of a gas attack. He was left unfit for active duty and transferred to the Entertainers Section of the British Army, where he served until the end of the war.

Priestley held the rank of officer when he left the army in 1919. He received a small grant to attend Cambridge University, where he studied Modern History and Political Science. Although he graduated with a degree, he was never comfortable with the life of an academic and decided to change direction.

In 1921, Priestley married Emily "Pat" Tempest, a librarian from Bradford, and together they began a new life in London. There they had two daughters, Barbara (1923) and Sylvia (1924), while Priestley established himself as a freelance non-fiction writer, completing numerous books and essays around this time. Tragically, Emily died of cancer in 1925, leaving Priestley to raise his daughters. He remarried a year later to Jane Wyndham Lewis, with whom he had two further daughters and a son.

Priestley collaborated with Hugh Walpole on his historical novel *Farthing Hall* in 1929, and its popularity gave him sufficient financial freedom and confidence to attempt his first solo novel. The result was *The Good Companions* which won the James Tait Black Memorial Prize for fiction. It was quickly followed by *Angel Pavement* in 1930, firmly establishing Priestley as a force within the literary world.

Priestley then turned his hand to writing plays. He collaborated on a stage adaptation of *The Good Companions*, and followed that with his first solo-authored play, *Dangerous Corner*, which opened in 1932 and was a great success. Rather than capitalise on this breakthrough, Priestley was soon travelling the country so that he could see first-hand the troubles experienced by industrial Britain during the recession. The result was a non-fiction publication, *English Journey*, which not only established Priestley as a social commentator, but also gave him themes that paved the way for his later works, including *An Inspector Calls*.

Shortly after the start of World War II, Priestley had another career change, becoming a broadcaster for the BBC. Attracting over 16 million listeners, Priestley felt that his broadcasts should try to boost moral during those difficult times by talking about how life would be after the war and by promoting traditional values. Despite his popularity (Priestley's shows had the highest listening figures of any radio programme aside from Churchill's speeches), the BBC cancelled his series of "Postscripts" after just a few months because the Ministry of Information believed he was too critical of the government.

Although he was a prolific writer across multiple disciplines, crafting plays, novels, essays, and several volumes of autobiography, Priestley tends to be remembered most for his intense dramas. Through his scripts he was able to couple his political beliefs with his deep interest in time theories, exploring how premonitions enable us to experience events before they occur. The finest example of this combination of themes is his 1945 masterpiece, *An Inspector Calls*. Interestingly, the play was first performed in Moscow, reaching London a year later in October 1946, where it enjoyed a long, successful run.

Priestley continued to balance his writing with his political and social responsibilities. He stood as an independent candidate in the 1945 general election but was not elected as a Member of Parliament, and from 1946-7 he was the British delegate at UNESCO conferences (United Nations Educational, Scientific and Cultural Organization). It was through UNESCO that he met the archaeologist and writer Jacquette Hawkes, whom Priestley married following his divorce from Jane in 1953. Later, spurred on by the nuclear testing of a hydrogen bomb in the Christmas Islands in 1957 (which he argued against in his essay "Britain and the Nuclear Bomb"), he became a founding member of the Campaign for Nuclear Disarmament (CND).

He wrote well into his seventies and remained generally active. The University of Bradford awarded him an honorary doctorate in 1970, and he was granted the freedom of the City of Bradford in 1973. In 1975 he opened the J.B. Priestley Library within the University of Bradford. Because of his strong socialist beliefs, he rejected offers of a knighthood, but in 1977 he accepted the Queen's Order of Merit because the honour had no political connections.

J.B. Priestley died on 14th August 1984, just 30 days before his 90th birthday, at his home in Stratford-upon-Avon. Fittingly, the City of Bradford erected a statue in his honour, which stands outside the National Media Museum in the centre of what has become the UNESCO City of Film.

# Page Creation

## 1. Script

The process starts with the writing of the script. The script describes the artwork for the artist to draw and also details the dialogue, captions and sound effects that will be added by the letterer. There are two editions of *An Inspector Calls*: Original Text and Quick Text. Both use the same artwork but feature different dialogue.

A page from the script of *An Inspector Calls* showing the two versions of the text.

## 2. Character Designs

While the scriptwriter is working on the panel descriptions, the artist can start work on designs for each character. He is striving to find a "look" for each individual that reflects his or her age and personality while making each person distinct to help the reader tell one from another.

## 3. Pencils

When creating the artwork for each page, the artist first creates a rough layout to check overall proportions, after which he creates a pencil drawing. He is considering many things during this process, including the pacing of the story, body language, character sizes, perspective, lettering space, texture and lighting. The page below is a superb example of Will capturing mood and tension while also putting over a sense of the passing of time.

The pencil drawing of page 131.

## 4. Inks

When completed, the pencil sketch is then inked. Inking is not simply tracing over the pencil sketch; it is the process of using black ink to fill in the shaded areas and to add clarity and cohesion to the pencilled artwork. Inking also adds texture and drama through shading and lighting, aiming all the time to retain the energy of the expressive pencils.

The inked page with pencil drawing removed.

## 5. Colouring

Adding colour really brings the page to life.

The finished artwork before lettering.

There is far more to the colouring stage than just replacing the white areas with colour. Some of the linework itself might be replaced with colour, also, the light sources are considered for shadows and highlights, and effects are added. Finally, the whole page is colour-balanced to match the other pages in the book.

## 6. Lettering

The final stage is to add the captions, sound effects, and speech bubbles from the script, which are laid on top of each coloured page. Two versions of each page are lettered, one for each of the two editions of the book (Original Text and Quick Text).

The lettered pages are then compiled into the finished books, ready for printing.

The finished page 131 with Original Text lettering.

# MORE TITLES AVAILABLE FROM

Classic Literature in a choice of 2 text versions. Simply choose the text version to match your reading level.

**Original Text** — THE CLASSIC NOVEL BROUGHT TO LIFE IN FULL COLOUR!
**Quick Text** — THE FULL STORY IN QUICK MODERN ENGLISH FOR A FAST-PACED READ!

## Jane Eyre: The Graphic Novel   (Charlotte Brontë)
- Script Adaptation: Amy Corzine • Artwork: John M. Burns
- Letters: Terry Wiley

ISBN: 978-1-906332-06-8

ISBN: 978-1-906332-08-2

"I scorn your idea of love and the counterfeit sentiment you offer. And I scorn you when you offer it."

• 144 Pages

## Frankenstein: The Graphic Novel   (Mary Shelley)
- Script Adaptation: Jason Cobley • Linework: Declan Shalvey • Art Direction: Jon Haward
- Colours: Jason Cardy & Kat Nicholson • Letters: Terry Wiley

ISBN: 978-1-906332-15-0

ISBN: 978-1-906332-16-7

"Cursed be the hands that formed you!"

• 144 Pages

## A Christmas Carol: The Graphic Novel   (Charles Dickens)
- Script Adaptation: Seán Michael Wilson • Pencils: Mike Collins
- Inks: David Roach • Colours: James Offredi • Letters: Terry Wiley

ISBN: 978-1-906332-17-4

ISBN: 978-1-906332-18-1

"I will honour Christmas in my heart, and try to keep it all the year. I will live in the Past, the Present, and the Future."

• 160 Pages

## Great Expectations: The Graphic Novel   (Charles Dickens)
- Script Adaptation: Jen Green • Linework: John Stokes • Colouring: Digikore Studios Ltd
- Colour Finishing: Jason Cardy • Letters: Jim Campbell

ISBN: 978-1-906332-09-9

ISBN: 978-1-906332-11-2

"I never saw my father or my mother, and never saw any likeness of either of them."

• 160 Pages

# OUR AWARD-WINNING RANGE

*"Classical Comics' graphic novels stand out way above others in the genre. The quality of the artwork is exceptional – the detail, relevance to the subject matter and the way they convey the emotions of the books are wonderful."*
Sarah Brew
www.parentsintouch.co.uk

*"The students have been really enthusiastic and the teachers have really enjoyed teaching them."*
Joanna Adkin, Senior Teacher

*"It's capturing the lightning in a different-shaped bottle. Amazing stuff!"*
Mike Carey, Novelist & Comic Writer

LOOK WHAT PEOPLE ARE SAYING ABOUT CLASSICAL COMICS.

## *The Canterville Ghost: The Graphic Novel* (Oscar Wilde)
- Script Adaptation: Seán Michael Wilson • Linework: Steve Bryant
- Colours: Jason Millet • Letters: Jim Campbell

ISBN: 978-1-906332-27-3

ISBN: 978-1-906332-28-0

*"Quick, quick," cried the Ghost, "or it will be too late."*

• 136 Pages

## *Wuthering Heights: The Graphic Novel* (Emily Brontë)
- Script Adaptation: Seán Michael Wilson • Artwork: John M. Burns
- Letters: Jim Campbell

ISBN: 978-1-906332-87-7

ISBN: 978-1-906332-88-4

*"That minx, Catherine Linton, or Earnshaw, or however she was called – wicked little soul!"*

• 160 Pages

## *Dracula: The Graphic Novel* (Bram Stoker)
- Script Adaptation: Jason Cobley • Linework: Staz Johnson
- Colours: James Offredi • Letters: Jim Campbell

ISBN: 978-1-906332-25-9

ISBN: 978-1-906332-26-6

*"I went down into the vaults. There lay the Count! He was either dead or asleep, I could not say which."*

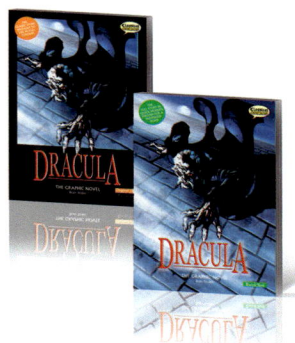

• 152 Pages

## *Sweeney Todd: The Graphic Novel* (Anonymous)
- Script Adaptation: Seán Michael Wilson • Linework: Declan Shalvey
- Colours: Jason Cardy & Kat Nicholson • Letters: Jim Campbell

ISBN: 978-1-906332-79-2

ISBN: 978-1-906332-80-8

*"Oh! to be sure, he came here, and I shaved him and polished him off."*

• 168 Pages

# SHAKESPEARE RANGE

Shakespeare's plays in a choice of 3 text versions. Simply choose the text version to match your reading level.

- **Original Text** — THE ENTIRE SHAKESPEARE PLAY - UNABRIDGED!
- **Plain Text** — THE ENTIRE PLAY TRANSLATED INTO PLAIN ENGLISH!
- **Quick Text** — THE ENTIRE PLAY IN QUICK MODERN ENGLISH FOR A FAST-PACED READ!

### Macbeth: The Graphic Novel   (William Shakespeare)
- Script Adaptation: John McDonald • Pencils: & Inks: Jon Haward
- Inking Assistant: Gary Erskine • Colours & Letters: Nigel Dobbyn
- • 144 Pages

 ISBN: 978-1-906332-03-7
 ISBN: 978-1-906332-04-4
 ISBN: 978-1-906332-05-1

### Romeo & Juliet: The Graphic Novel   (William Shakespeare)
- Script Adaptation: John McDonald • Linework: Will Volley
- Colours: Jim Devlin • Letters: Jim Campbell
- • 168 Pages

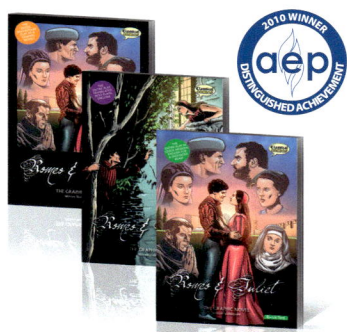
 ISBN: 978-1-906332-19-8
 ISBN: 978-1-906332-20-4
 ISBN: 978-1-906332-21-1

### The Tempest: The Graphic Novel   (William Shakespeare)
- Script Adaptation: John McDonald • Pencils: Jon Haward
- Inks: Gary Erskine • Colours: & Letters: Nigel Dobbyn
- • 144 Pages

 ISBN: 978-1-906332-29-7
 ISBN: 978-1-906332-30-3
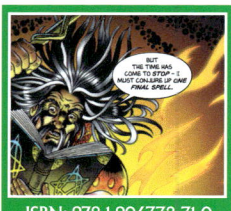 ISBN: 978-1-906332-31-0

### A Midsummer Night's Dream: The Graphic Novel   (William Shakespeare)
- Script Adaptation: John McDonald • Characters & Artwork: Kat Nicholson & Jason Cardy
- Letters: Jim Campbell
- • 144 Pages

 ISBN: 978-1-906332-89-1
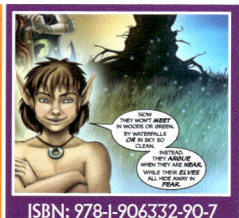 ISBN: 978-1-906332-90-7
 ISBN: 978-1-906332-91-4

To see the complete range, and to view samples online, go to www.classicalcomics.com